THE COURTAULD SILVER

Frontispiece Trade card of Samuel Courtauld, probably engraved in 1751 when he moved to Cornhill.

The Courtauld Silver

An Introduction to the Work of the
Courtauld Family of Goldsmiths

J. F. HAYWARD

Sotheby Parke Bernet Publications
London & New York

© Courtaulds, Limited 1975

Produced and published in Great Britain by
Sotheby Parke Bernet Publications Limited,
36 Dover Street, London W1X 3RB

Edition for the United States of America distributed by
Sotheby Parke Bernet Publications,
81 Adams Drive, Totowa, New Jersey 07512

ISBN 0 85667 018 9

Designed by Paul Sharp

Printed and bound in Great Britain by W. S. Cowell Limited,
Ipswich

Contents

Acknowledgements

We should like to thank the following for permission to reproduce their photographs:

The Corporation of the City of London, Plate 16

Courtaulds Limited, Plates 10, 11, 12, 13, 14, 15, 17, 18, 19, 20, 21, 22, 23, 24, 25, 26, 29, 30, 31, 32, 33 and 35

The Worshipful Company of Clothworkers, Plate 27

The Worshipful Company of Goldsmiths, Plates 1, 2, 3, 4, 5, 8 and 28

The Victoria and Albert Museum, Plate 34

List of Plates

John Hayward was a Deputy Keeper in the Victoria and Albert Museum and is now an Associate Director of Sotheby's, the Fine Art Auctioneers. He is a leading authority on antique silver and is the author of *Huguenot Silver in England* and of numerous books on the applied arts. He is a Liveryman of the Worshipful Company of Goldsmiths and has arranged and written the catalogues of a series of exhibitions of English silver both in London and abroad.

The following account is in part based on *Some Silver Wrought by the Courtauld Family of London Goldsmiths in the eighteenth century* by E. Alfred Jones, privately printed at the Shakespeare Head Press, Oxford, in 1940.

The Courtauld Silver

Members of the Courtauld family and the firm of Courtaulds Limited have in the course of the last fifty years assembled a collection of the work of their goldsmith predecessors. This collection has grown to such an extent that, apart from minor gaps, it now covers the whole range of their production. Three generations of the Courtauld family worked in London as practising goldsmiths during the eighteenth century; between them they covered the period from 1701, when the first member, Augustin, was apprenticed, until 1780 when his grandson, Samuel, sold the business and emigrated to America. The following account records something of their history and assesses their importance in the craft they so long pursued.

The Courtaulds were active at a time when the goldsmithing trade in England was enjoying the most flourishing period in its history. The eighteenth century saw a great increase in the wealth of the country; the Crown, peers and commoners, landowners and men of affairs, Whigs and Tories, all were great patrons of the goldsmiths. Great wealth was brought home to England by many who had made their fortunes in India or the Colonies and much of this was invested in silver; at the same time there were important commissions from the City Companies and the churches. The opportunities brought skilful craftsmen and gifted designers into the London trade, and the standard of workmanship achieved in this century has never been surpassed. Although vast quantities of eighteenth-century silver have been melted for refashioning, the surviving pieces are innumerable and the work of one single family, such as the Courtaulds, can still be studied in a large number of examples. Not only was a fine service of plate an indispensable status symbol, it was also a normal method of investing surplus capital. This aspect of silver vessels as a form of specie is emphasised in the way in which the eighteenth-century goldsmith presented his bill, which specified the weight of the piece as so many ounces and then charged a variable price per ounce according to the amount of work required for fashioning (i.e. for making up).

During most of the century London was the main centre of the craft. The goldsmiths of the ancient provincial cities, such as Exeter, Norwich or Bristol, ceased to compete with those of the Capital and it was not till the last quarter of the century that the Birmingham masters began to offer serious competition.

The Courtaulds were a Huguenot family from near the small town of St. Pierre in the Ile d'Oleron off La Rochelle, the historic stronghold of French Protestantism. They left their homeland and came to England along with many thousands of their compatriots to escape religious persecution. This had become increasingly intense during the reign of Louis XIV and had culminated in the year 1685 in the Revocation of the Edict of Nantes, the Royal Proclamation which, since 1598, had guaranteed the Huguenots freedom of worship, along with many other privileges. Such was the brutality of the persecution that the only alternatives to emigration were either abjuration of the Protestant faith or execution, condemnation to service as a galley-slave or imprisonment.

The Huguenots formed a closed community in London, living in restricted areas, mainly Soho and Spitalfields, worshipping in their own churches and intermarrying. This exclusiveness may not have been altogether of their own choice. Although at first their plight aroused great sympathy in England, they numbered many highly skilled masters and their competition was far from welcome to native craftsmen working in the same trades. They were enabled to settle in England and to follow their own trades by an Order in Council of Charles II in 1681, which granted Letters of Denization under the Great Seal (i.e. naturalisation) free of charge.

The competition to which the London goldsmiths were subjected was a serious threat to their livelihood. Although most of the Huguenots came, like the Courtaulds, from the provincial towns and not from Paris, the fashion in silversmithing that they offered their English customers was far in advance of that current amongst the London goldsmiths. The latter were still working in the Restoration style, an English version of the florid Dutch baroque. This called for elaborate decoration by the techniques of embossing and chasing but showed a deficient sense of proportion. The Huguenots offered a more sophisticated style which went back to classical standards of proportion and used ornament with more taste and discretion. This style, which had been worked out by the Court artists of Louis XIV, was soon accepted and emulated throughout western Europe by all who made any claim to keep up with fashion. It was the ability of the Huguenot goldsmiths to work in a manner that was novel, sophisticated and at the same time highly decorative that brought them the great success they quickly achieved in London.

This success brought determined resistance from the London trade; life was not made easy for the Huguenots and they had reasons more pressing than their common language to compel them to keep together. Repeated efforts were made through the Goldsmiths' Company to limit the foreign competition. As early as 1682 and again in 1683 representations were made to the Company against the 'great numbers of alien goldsmiths that are permitted to work in and about London'. At this time only two Huguenots had been admitted to the Freedom of the Company and thereby allowed to set up their workshops within the City. The most serious complaint came in 1711 when a petition to the Court of the Company was signed by no fewer than 53 members, including some of the leading London masters. This claimed that 'by the admittance of necessitous strangers, whose desperate fortunes obliged them to work at miserable rates, the representing members have been forced to bestow much more time and labour in working up their plate than hath been the practice of former times, when the prices of workmanship were greater'. This rather disingenuous protest reveals that the Huguenot goldsmiths had improved the standard of work in the trade while at the same time lowering the prices charged.

Augustin Courtauld the elder, father of the goldsmith of that name, was the first of the family to arrive in England – at some date between 1687 and 1689. He was the eldest surviving son of Pierre Courtauld, who abjured the Protestant faith and remained in France. Pierre was a merchant and Augustin followed the same trade in France. In London the latter eventually became a cooper, but two of his sons became goldsmiths. The eldest, named Augustin after his father, was born in France about 1686 and was granted Letters of Denization on July 20, 1696. He was apprenticed at the usual age of about fourteen on August 9, 1701 to Simon Pantin of St. Martin's Lane, London. Pantin was also of Huguenot origin, and had only recently established himself as a master goldsmith, having first entered his mark at Goldsmiths' Hall in the same year, 1701. Augustin Courtauld was thus one of his earliest apprentices. Pantin had in turn been apprenticed to yet another Huguenot goldsmith, Pierre Harache, the first of the *immigré* craftsmen to gain admittance to the Worshipful Company of Goldsmiths and thereby obtain the right to set up shop within the City of London. The majority of the Huguenots, like Simon Pantin, preferred, however, to work in the West End of London, where large numbers of their compatriots in many other trades eventually settled.

Augustin served his seven years of apprenticeship under Simon Pantin from 1701 to 1708; he was then made a Freeman of the Goldsmiths' Company and set up in the latter year as a plate-worker in Church Court off St. Martin's Lane. He remained there for twenty-one years, until 1729, when he moved to better premises in Chandos Street in the same neighbourhood. He chose as his mark the first two letters of his name, CO with a fleur-de-lis above within a three-lobed punch (pl 1). In choosing the fleur-de-lis he was doubtless referring to his French origin; many other Huguenot goldsmiths registered marks in which a crown or a fleur-de-lis, both standard features of French goldsmiths' marks, were introduced. Augustin used this mark after 1720, when, following upon the reintroduction of the old Sterling standard in place of the higher Britannia standard, he should have registered a new mark, consisting of the initials of his christian and his surname, for silver of the lower standard. He continued, however, to use the higher standard and the older mark until 1729, when he registered a second mark, the fleur-de-lis surmounting his initials AC for Sterling standard (pl 2). After 1729 most of his work was executed in the lower standard. In 1739 it was found that the use of two different marks by the same goldsmith, one for the Britannia and one for the Sterling standard, led to confusion and the Goldsmiths' Company instructed all its members to destroy their existing marks and enter a single one to a different design. In that year accordingly, Augustin entered his third and last mark, his initials in script capitals with the fleur-de-lis below (pl 3).

At this point mention should be made of the second Courtauld goldsmith, Peter. A son of Augustin the elder by his second marriage, Peter was born in England in 1690 and was, like his half-brother, apprenticed to Simon Pantin. His apprenticeship lasted from 1705 until 1712, during which time he married a member of his master's family. Though he was entered as a Freeman of the Goldsmiths' Company in 1712, Peter Courtauld did not register his own mark (pl 4) until 1721, presumably because he was still employed by Simon Pantin. He lived until 1729 but no piece of silver made by him has yet been identified.

It is a striking fact that a very high proportion of the really important silver vessels made during the last decade of the seventeenth century and the first quarter of the eighteenth century was produced by Huguenots. As the Huguenots became Anglicised, however, they lost their predominance in the trade and by the second quarter of the eighteenth century only two names, those of Paul de Lamerie and Paul Crespin, stand out well above those of the indigenous goldsmiths. While an early arrival, Pierre Harache, received many commissions from the most influential and wealthy members of the English nobility, his pupil, Simon Pantin, had a somewhat less distinguished clientele. His production consists of pieces of exquisite proportion and great purity of form, but for the most part they lack the magnificent cast and chased ornament found on the finer pieces made by his master. Presumably the whole of his apprenticeship had been passed in London and he had become aware of the national taste for simplicity, which has always re-asserted itself after each wave of foreign influence has died away. Like Simon Pantin, Augustin Courtauld did not succeed in obtaining the most important commissions. He seems to have been content to follow the manner of his master, producing silver of excellent design and proportion. His earlier pieces could easily be mistaken for Pantin's work and his whole production displays a reticence which prevents his work from standing out above the general level of taste and craftsmanship of the time. In estimating the status of an eighteenth-century goldsmith one must not judge by modern standards. Fashion changes so rapidly now that the merit of a craftsman tends to be judged by his ability to keep up with the competition for new ideas and methods of presentation. In the eighteenth century fashion was more stable and it was less essential for the goldsmith to seek novelty at any price. The fact that Augustin Courtauld's silver does not present any striking difference from that of most of his contemporaries would not at the time have been regarded as constituting serious grounds for criticism. In the bulk of his production he followed the English manner, relying for his effect upon the qualities of texture and form natural to the material which he faultlessly designed and wrought. Most of his work shows broad areas of plain surface framed within simple mouldings rather than the rich ornamentation of the Louis XIV style which had been favoured by the previous generation of Huguenot goldsmiths. He lived to what would in the eighteenth century have been regarded as a great age – sixty-five – and worked in the craft for forty-five years from his apprenticeship in 1701 to 1746, when his son, Samuel, took over. Augustin enjoyed considerable success as a goldsmith and when he died in April 1751 he left a sum of £2,000, as well as other small bequests and a residuary estate consisting of his house, tools of the trade, furniture, etc. The figure of £2,000 should be multiplied by some thirty or more times to arrive at a modern equivalent.

Augustin is represented in the Courtaulds collection by pieces dating between 1710, two years after he became a master of his craft, and 1745, six years before his death. Before looking at his works further one or two mistaken attributions must be dispelled. During the first half of the eighteenth century certain goldsmiths specialised in the production of miniature vessels in silver intended for use in dolls' houses. These miniatures were exact reproductions of the full-size vessels and they were made with great care. Through the misreading of a maker's mark many of these miniatures, actually made by the London goldsmith David Clayton, have been mistakenly attributed to Augustin Courtauld. He has also been wrongly credited with having made one of the most magnificent pieces of silver in the Royal Collection at Windsor Castle. This is a vast centrepiece of no less than 85 lbs weight which bears, in fact, the mark of another goldsmith of French extraction, Paul Crespin. It was commissioned for Frederick, Prince of Wales, and delivered in 1741.

The standard piece of presentation plate in the eighteenth century was a large two-handled cup with separate cover surmounted by a knob finial. Such pieces could be used as loving-cups or as sideboard ornaments. Augustin produced a handsome series of these for different customers and they provide a most convincing evidence of his powers (pl 17). Some of the cups he made are of distinctly robust form, but for the most part he seems to have specialised in vessels intended for use on the tea-table (pls 10, 13, 14, 18, 19) rather than in those more massive vessels that might have enabled him to work on the monumental scale associated with the finest Huguenot work. This should not be regarded as a reflection of his own personal taste; it was doubtless forced upon him by economic circumstance.

While some of the earlier Huguenots, such as Pierre Harache or Pierre Platel, had numbered amongst their clients many members of the English aristocracy, Augustin drew upon the gentry for the majority of his commissions. It is true that he made a two-handled cup and cover for the Earl of Godolphin, but for the most part he was working for customers to whom questions of cost would carry great weight. The massive cast ornament favoured by the Huguenots would have put up the price of plate considerably, especially at that period when the weight of precious metal used in a piece represented a far higher proportion of the final cost than it would now. Augustin often preferred to use the restrained square or octagonal forms (pls 11, 14) which, though introduced by the Huguenots, had been taken up with enthusiasm by the English-born goldsmiths. When he did make use of typical Huguenot ornament, such as vertical applied straps, he did so with marked discretion. The straps (pls 12, 17) are widely spaced and the handles of his cups lack the bold sculptural treatment favoured by the earlier Huguenots.

While the bulk of Augustin Courtauld's large production conformed to the usual designs of the time, he did from time to time make a piece of outstanding beauty in which nobility of form was enhanced by a restrained use of ornament. Amongst these may be included the chocolate-pot with its superbly modelled pear-shaped body (pl 13) and a covered cup in which he made unusually skilful use of superimposed layers of cut ornament, set against a matted border to give contrast of texture. Augustin rarely made such florid use of applied leaves and straps as his Huguenot contemporaries; as a rule he preferred the simple lanceolate leaves (pls 12, 17) of the type that had been employed by Platel some twenty years earlier. Only on a two-handled cup of 1718 and on the State Salt of the Mansion House (pl 16) does he introduce them in their most sophisticated form, the upper surfaces chased with shells or heads and interlacing strap-work. To judge by the many surviving examples bearing his mark, Augustin was a great maker of trays and salvers; at first sight these may appear to be pieces of minor importance, but in fact the making and application of the complex, shaped borders (pl 15) called for the highest technical skill.

The Court of the Emperors of Russia was an important customer of the Huguenot goldsmiths of London during the first half of the eighteenth century. The most spectacular purchase was a huge service bought in London for the Empress Catherine I in, or about, the year 1725. When the service was inventoried in 1734 it consisted of 36 pieces of gilt plate and 329 of white plate. Only a fraction of the original service has been preserved in Russia, but most of these vessels bear the marks of Huguenot goldsmiths of London. Augustin's mark does not appear on any of the surviving pieces of this service but he is represented by two interesting pieces of silver in Russia. The first is a silver tea-table in the Kremlin bearing the London hall-mark for 1742. The circumstances in which this table reached Russia are not recorded. It may have been a gift from George II, but the absence of both his coat-of-arms and that of the Russian Imperial house makes this unlikely. The top is engraved with elaborate borders of late baroque design enclosing human heads, but has no heraldic decoration of any sort. By this date silver furniture was no longer fashionable in England; earlier in the century the nobility had rivalled the Crown in purchasing such opulent pieces, but by the 1740s the precious metal had given way to exotic woods such as mahogany and padouk in which the London cabinet-makers were achieving such magnificent effects. Though clearly an expensive article, a silver table was less extravagant than might at first appear. It was constructed of sheet silver of light gauge which was nailed to a simple wooden carcase. Very little hammer work was called for, but such a piece gave great scope to the artist who had to enliven its extensive plain surfaces with engraving. Only the very largest establishments would have had an engraver on the staff; most goldsmiths put out their work for engraving to a specialist in that art. This led to a certain sameness in eighteenth-century silver because one engraver would have worked for many different goldsmiths. The standard was, on the other hand, very high, and Augustin must have employed one of the leading masters in the art, for the engraving on his pieces is excellently proportioned to the space available and delicately executed (pls 15, 18). The second example of Augustin's work in Russia is in the Hermitage; this is a plain inkstand made in the year 1730. It is of standard design and one wonders how such comparatively simple pieces came to be ordered for the far-off Court of Russia. It is hardly likely to have been specially commissioned; perhaps a Russian ambassador in London acquired it for the use of his embassy and it was subsequently returned to Russia.

Augustin's most imposing surviving work is the State Salt of the Corporation of the City of London at the Mansion House (pl 16). This splendid piece of plate was originally made in 1730 for a private individual and was only presented eleven years later to the Sword Bearer of the Corporation and 'to his successors for the use of their table at the Lord Mayor's, 1741'. This piece is the last of the great ceremonial salts to be made in England; it is also the only surviving piece made by Augustin Courtauld in which striking originality is to be found. Its curious form is due to the retention of the scroll branches above the receptacle for salt. The purpose of the scrolls was to support a napkin to keep the salt clean before the meal and a dish of dessert after the salt was done with; usual on seventeenth-century salts, scrolls were archaic by the date this one was made. From the bowl of the salt below each scroll springs a dolphin foot; such features usually had some symbolic significance and in this case the connection doubtless relates to the salt in the ocean. Nicholas Sprimont, the Liège-born goldsmith who came to England in about 1740 and registered his mark for the first time in 1742, produced some admirable salts for Frederick, Prince of Wales, the designs of which were based on shellfish and other marine creatures, both natural and mythical. The dolphin foot also appears on another model of salt by Augustin Courtauld, though this is of otherwise very modest nature. Presumably in expectation of the hard use his scroll salt was likely to receive, Augustin has fitted a ring within the base to strengthen the feet – an unhappy feature from the point of view of the design, but doubtless necessary to enable the piece to stand up to the rigours of use on the banqueting table. The body of the salt is decorated with applied lambrequins cast and chased with shells and strapwork. This particular ornament was of French origin and constituted one of the more lasting contributions of the Huguenots to English fashion in silver. Whereas most other features of Huguenot design were forgotten or abandoned as no longer fashionable, as the French goldsmiths who had introduced them died off, this was one of the details that was taken over by the English craftsmen.

During the years between 1730 and 1740 a process of great importance in the history of English silver was taking place; the development of the rococo style. Ever since the close of the Middle Ages, English silver design has been based on the classical principle of symmetry and now, for the short space of some thirty years, asymmetrical design was fashionable, in so far as the form and function of the various silver vessels would permit. Not only was symmetry abandoned, but the whole range of classical ornament, which had dominated design since the Renaissance, gave way to compositions of abstract scrollwork combined with grotesque creatures and naturalistic forms such as leaves, flowers and animals. Silver vessels were no longer constructed according to an architectural plan with clearly marked vertical and horizontal members; instead the design was conceived as a whole with each part flowing rhythmically into the next.

Another Huguenot, Paul de Lamerie, was at the forefront of the new fashion but Augustin did not follow his lead. He continued to take a firmly conservative attitude and ignored the new style long after it had been generally adopted by his contemporaries. Though Augustin Courtauld was making silver until 1746, and possibly even later, only one piece bearing his mark and made in the rococo fashion is recorded. It is probable that this was the work of his son, Samuel, who was employed in his shop when it was made. The piece is a cake-basket of 1744 (pl 20), in which the turbulent forms and ordered confusion of rococo are well mastered.

Among the various apprentices, all of Huguenot descent, taken by Augustin was his second son, Samuel, who was born in 1720. He entered his father's workshop at the age of fourteen and, after serving his seven years apprenticeship, continued as a journeyman for another five years, until 1746, when he registered his mark, the initials S.C. under a sun in splendour within a three-lobed punch (pl 5). During this period he must have worked upon many of the coffee-pots, trays and the like which bear his father's mark. In 1746 he set up under his own name and, as he occupied his father's premises in Chandos Street off St. Martin's Lane, it is probable that he took over his father's business. He stayed there until 1751, when, upon the death of his father, he moved to 21 Cornhill, in the City of London. He had received all his father's tools and patterns as well as £400 in cash and the move was presumably based on his new-found prosperity. He died suddenly at the early age of forty-five.

As one might expect, Samuel did not delay in taking up the new fashion to which his father had been so unsympathetic. The tea-kettle and stand of 1748 (pl 21) shows a marked contrast to his father's manner, while the tea-caddy and sauce-boat of 1750 (pls 22, 23) already show the influence of Paul de Lamerie. This can be seen in the modelling of the feet with their upper termination formed as a plump-cheeked cherub's head. In the immediately following years Samuel showed himself to be a complete master of this exacting style. A centre-piece and magnificent tureen both hall-marked in 1751 (pls 25, 26) show how complete was his appreciation of the possibilities of rococo design. This rococo style, which determined the course of fashion during the whole of Samuel Courtauld's working life, gave unlimited opportunity to the skilled and inventive designer.

Freed from the tyranny of symmetry and classical proportion, able to express their individuality in the choice and composition of ornament, the goldsmiths of the mid-eighteenth century were limited only by the resources of their own imagination and by the intrinsic qualities of the precious metal they used. Samuel did, however, inherit his father's appreciation of the merits of the metal he used and some of his vessels, such as the coffee-pot of 1760 (pl 29), are presented as pure form with no more ornamentation than the simple mouldings and a scrolled spout. A complete contrast can be seen in the little tea-caddy of 1750, the whole surface of which is conceived as a composition of curves and scrolls from which scenes and figures develop (pl 22). Samuel Courtauld seems to have achieved much the same status as his father in the London trade. He evidently numbered some of the aristocracy amongst his clientele but most of his orders came from the gentry. He did not reach the top flight of goldsmiths of his generation, but his early death at the age of forty-five must be taken into consideration when estimating his importance. In 1763 Samuel Courtauld was admitted to the Livery of the Goldsmiths' Company, an incident that implies recognition of his status in the craft, but his advance in the Company was cut off by his death in 1765. He is represented among the Company plate by a most remarkable coffee-urn of 1760, the pear-shaped body of which is embossed in high relief with chinoiserie subjects set within a riotous rococo framework (pl 28), and by a salver, also of 1760, with a pierced border. This salver was presented to the Company by George Courtauld, a direct descendant, in 1952 when a member of the Court of Assistants of the Company. Like his father, Samuel produced many coffee-pots of excellent design according to the fashion of the period, but he was also capable of making pieces outside the usual repertoire of the goldsmith. In 1755 he was commissioned by the Court of another City Company, the Clothworkers, to make a new head for their Beadle's staff. This he designed in high rococo style (pl 27); the knob of the staff is chased with asymmetrical scrollwork and festoons of flowers enclosing panels with the arms of the City of London and scenes symbolic of cloth-working. This is surmounted by the arms and crest of the Company with supporters modelled in the round, quite a masterpiece of its kind. Samuel Courtauld's sympathy with and understanding of rococo is also shown by the design of his trade-card (frontispiece). This describes him as a jeweller as well as a goldsmith and claims that he 'makes and sells all sorts of Plate, Jewels, Watches and all other curious work in Gold and Silver'. Though he doubtless retailed both jewellery and watches, it is unlikely that he would also have manufactured them, such work being the province of specialist masters.

Among Samuel Courtauld's finest works are his toilet services, then a usual wedding present given by a bridegroom. They consisted of a dozen or more articles with a silver-framed mirror as the centre-piece, and were supplied in a leather-covered fitted case. Since they included a variety of objects, some of which, such as snuffers and candlesticks, were made by specialist craftsmen, it is usual to find more than one goldsmith represented. Samuel Courtauld had a part in the toilet service which was made for the Empress Elisabeth of Russia (1741–1761). When it was listed in the 1908 inventory of the Russian Imperial Collection in the Winter Palace, the service was composed of thirty-five pieces, of which seven bore Samuel Courtauld's mark, all dating from 1757 or 1758. Three other Huguenot goldsmiths were represented in the service, Elias Cachat, Daniel Piers and Pierre Gillois. A jewel casket and two boxes from another service were sold in Russia in 1933. The casket is of such distinction as to rank as Samuel's finest surviving piece. A striking feature is the superlative embossed work, the top being decorated with a scene of the Toilet of Venus within a scroll-work frame. The embossing was probably the work of a specialist craftsman, not Samuel Courtauld himself, but the credit for the conception of the piece should presumably be given to him. This service dates from the year 1763 and shows strong French influence, not in the earlier Huguenot style but in a more up-to-date one derived from the fashion of the Court of Louis XV. At this date the short-lived rococo style was already giving way to another rebirth of classical taste in France, but in this London-made casket one still sees a most elegant and sophisticated expression of the rococo.

When Samuel Courtauld died in 1765, after only nineteen years in the craft, he left the business to his widow, Louisa Perina, who was then in her mid-thirties. In 1765/6 she registered her own mark, the initials LC in a lozenge-shaped punch (pl 6), at the Goldsmiths' Hall and carried on the business. This does not mean, as some romantically inclined persons have maintained, that the lady herself set to work at the bench. She would have inherited from her late husband not only the goodwill, the stock-in-trade and the tools but also the journeymen and apprentices. Whatever part was played by Louisa Perina Courtauld is not likely to have gone beyond the sphere of the counting-house. The death of Samuel Courtauld came at a time when fashion was changing and the widow was probably unable to cope with the triple task of running a thriving business, bringing up four children and introducing a new style. She was, however, assisted by a former apprentice of her late husband, George Cowles, who within a few months of his master's death was made a Freeman of the Goldsmiths' Company by service, 'with the consent of Louisa Perina Courtauld, the widow and Extrix.' Three years later in 1768 Cowles was taken on as a partner in the business and in the same year he married Judith Jacobs, a grand-daughter of Augustin and niece of his late master. A few pieces struck with the mark of Louisa Courtauld are known, among them the two-handled cup (pl 31) which offers a tolerable solution of the awkward problem of reconciling rococo form with the recently introduced neo-classical decoration. A new mark was registered by Louisa Courtauld and George Cowles, the initials LC over GC in a rectangle (pl 7). It is not possible to reproduce the entries of the marks of Louisa Courtauld of 1765/6 and of Louisa Courtauld and George Cowles of 1769 as the relevant volume covering registration of marks at Goldsmiths' Hall between 1758 and 1773 is missing. This volume was sent in 1773 for the information of the Parliamentary Committee examining hall-marking and it was apparently never returned. It is believed to have been burnt in the fire that destroyed the Houses of Parliament in 1834.

The neo-classical revival re-introduced symmetry and the old-established principles of proportion but expressed them in a lighter, less pompous mood than that which had informed silver of the first third of the century. A comparison between the two-handled cup of 1731 (pl 17) and that made by Louisa Perina Courtauld and George Cowles in 1770 (pl 32) well illustrates the change of mood. The later cup is far more elegant and the delicate ornament makes it more attractive. It will be seen that the rococo interval, during which so much value had been placed on ornament, had not passed without leaving some trace and the silver vessels made in the neo-classical style in England are altogether more decorative than the ponderous pieces made half a century before. The neo-classical style established itself relatively slowly in the goldsmiths' trade and many of the pieces made in the late 1760's and 1770's show a rather conflicting marriage of rococo liveliness and neo-classical discipline. The cup of 1770 (pl 32) is also remarkable by reason of the novel features it introduces; these include bright-cut engraving and inset cast panels of classical figure subjects derived from antique vases. It is a most advanced piece for its date and shows impressive progress in comparison with the rococo teapot (pl 30) produced in the Courtauld workshop in the year of Samuel's death.

The Louisa Courtauld and George Cowles partnership was no more a leader of fashion than were the other goldsmith members of the family, but it certainly mastered the new style. Their skill has been well described by Robert Rowe in his book on Adam silver: 'To Louisa Courtauld and George Cowles neo-classicism seems quickly to have become a natural way of expressing themselves as artists. They had an extraordinary knack of using a charming variation on a familiar motif in just the right place and of contrasting an area of decoration with the most complementary amount of plain surface. The cup of 1771 (pl 34) shows off their skill very well. The eye delights in the flowing frieze, every other flower in which is reversed with its stem making an extra spiral in the design; the frilliness of the acanthus leaves is subtly emphasised too by the reflecting powers of the plain convexity of the cup.'

The partnership between Louisa Perina Courtauld and George Cowles lasted for nine years, coming to an end in 1777 when Cowles' place was taken by Louisa's elder son, Samuel Courtauld. A new mark consisting of their combined initials (pl 8) was registered at Goldsmiths' Hall and a few pieces bearing this mark exist. By the time that the last Courtauld partnership was established the neo-classical style had been purified of all trace of the rococo and had developed an elegant but somewhat dry and academic manner. It is this manner that pervades the small group of silver made by the Courtaulds between 1777 and 1780. The most important piece by them is a large gilt two-handled cup, now belonging to the Courtauld family, with the London hall-mark for 1778. It bears the arms of John Fitzgibbon (1748–1804), who later became Lord Chancellor of Ireland. The arms are surmounted by a baron's coronet and, as Fitzgibbon was not created a baronet in the Irish Peerage until 1789, he may have bought the cup second-hand. This last change was not a fortunate one, for the new partnership persisted for only three years. In 1780 the business and the premises in Cornhill were sold to another goldsmith, John Henderson, and the Courtaulds ceased to make silver.

Little is known of the younger Samuel Courtauld, who was twenty-five years old when he entered the business. He took up his Freedom of the Goldsmiths' Company on March 4, 1778, but abandoned it within two years and emigrated to America. Although he registered a mark with his mother, he may not have been any more familiar with the craft than she was and may have concerned himself exclusively with the business side of the firm. In America he became a successful merchant and died in 1821.

It was not unusual in the eighteenth century for a craft to persist through several generations of the same family, but the record of the Courtaulds in producing silver of fine quality and impeccable design over eighty years during the most flourishing and creative period in the history of the craft in this country is surely unequalled.

The Plates

1   Augustin Courtauld, first mark, Britannia standard, registered at Goldsmiths' Hall on December 23, 1708

2   Augustin Courtauld, second mark, Sterling standard, registered at Goldsmiths' Hall on October 7, 1729

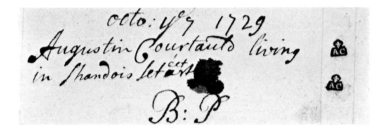

3   Augustin Courtauld, third mark, Sterling standard, registered at Goldsmiths' Hall on July 6, 1739

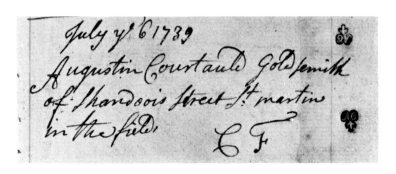

4   Peter Courtauld, first and second marks, registered at Goldsmiths' Hall on
    June 15 and July 21, 1721. No piece by him has ever been identified

5   Samuel Courtauld the elder, first and second marks, registered at Goldsmiths'
    Hall on October 6, 1746 and November 23, 1751

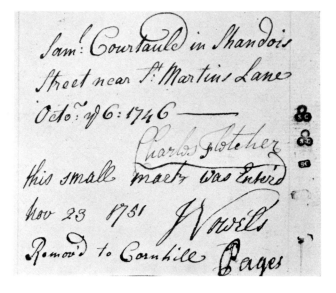

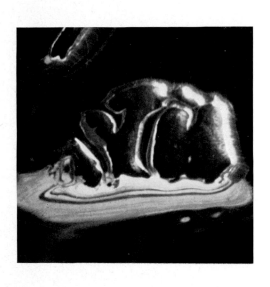

6 Louisa Courtauld, mark in use from 1766 to 1768

7 Louisa Courtauld and George Cowles, mark in use from 1768 to 1777

8 Louisa Courtauld and Samuel Courtauld the younger, mark registered at Goldsmiths' Hall on October 16, 1777

9a   Detail showing full set of marks on a strawberry dish by Augustin Courtauld, Britannia standard, London, 1720

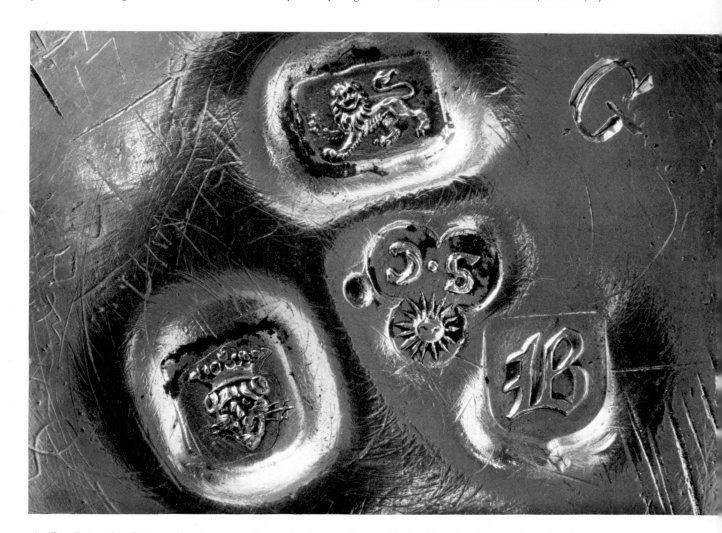

9b   Detail showing full set of marks on a coffee-pot by Samuel Courtauld the elder, Sterling standard, London, 1757

36

10   Coffee-pot, Augustin Courtauld, Britannia standard, 1713

11   Tapersticks, Augustin Courtauld, Britannia standard, 1718

12   Sugar-castor, Augustin Courtauld, Britannia standard, 1721

13   Chocolate-pot, Augustin Courtauld, Britannia standard, 1723

14   Set of tea-caddies with silver-mounted case, Augustin Courtauld, Britannia standard, 1723

15   Salver, Augustin Courtauld, Britannia standard, 1728

16   The State Salt of the Sword Bearer of the City of London, Augustin Courtauld, 1730

17   Two-handled cup and cover, Augustin Courtauld, Britannia standard, 1731

18   Coffee-pot, Augustin Courtauld, 1733

19   Sugar-box, Augustin Courtauld, 1737

20   Cake-basket, Augustin Courtauld, 1745

21   Tea-kettle and stand, Samuel Courtauld, 1748

22   Tea-caddy, Samuel Courtauld, 1750

23   One of a pair of sauce-boats, Samuel Courtauld, 1750

24   Inkstand, Samuel Courtauld, 1750

25   Centre-piece, Samuel Courtauld, 1751

26   Soup-tureen, Samuel Courtauld, 1751

27   Beadle's staff of the Worshipful Company of Clothworkers, Samuel Courtauld, 1755

28   Coffee-urn, Samuel Courtauld, 1760

29   Coffee-pot, Samuel Courtauld, 1760

30   Teapot, Louisa Courtauld, 1765

31   Two-handled cup and cover, Louisa Courtauld, 1765

32   Cup and cover, Louisa Courtauld and George Cowles, 1770

33   Covered vase, Louisa Courtauld and George Cowles, 1771

34 Two-handled cup and cover, Louisa Courtauld and George Cowles, 1771
(Victoria and Albert Museum, Crown copyright)

35   Teapot, Louisa Courtauld and George Cowles, 1773